This Guide has been written as an ɛ
Witches Runes

Going forward we encourage you to pursue your
own Methods, Theology and Practices.

Every time you delve, do so with a clear
head and clearer intentions.

Trust in your gut and
Remain open minded.

What are Witches Runes?

Witches Runes are a modern equivalent to their ancient predecessors. Using symbols, messages are channelled through the practitioner, guiding them to advice, warnings and general enlightenment. Whether this is by connections to ancestors or our own higher selves, the runes allow us to bridge the connection and ultimately find answers to questions we need to know.

How to use Witches Runes

Drawing/Pulling Runes can be done in many ways and looking online you can find many methods. Ultimately, we suggest that you do this in whatever way feels natural to you.

We have given some suggestions, feel free to give them a go. Remember what ever results you get, go with your gut. What isn't obvious now may become clear later. Equally don't jump to conclusions, let time unfold the truth.

The Spread

A spread is the term used to refer to the order in which
you pull your Runes and the questions you are asking.
The most common spread used with Tarot Practitioners
and Rune Readers alike is referred to as

PAST-PRESENT-FUTURE

Three Runes are drawn in this order and the results read
accordingly, being obvious in their request these are pulled often
to give advice on general living.
Some prefer answers to be more progressive from this asking

PAST-PRESENT-FUTURE-AIDS-HINDRANCES

The follow up looks for what can help with a situation
and what could cause issues along the way.

Pulling the Runes

How to draw Runes is also considered personal so choose
your own method, but here is a couple of suggestions.

Open your Runes Satchel, close your eyes and focus on your
question. While doing this take in a long breath then exhale into
the Satchel blowing the question from your mind into the bag.
Once you have done this, blindly pull the Runes
in the order of your chosen spread.
Another method is having a cloth down empty the Rune
bag, close your eyes and lift the Runes intuitively this
is a popular method feeling authentic to many.

Charging Runes

Prior to using your runes it is recommended that they be placed on a charging plate, our plate of choice is one made out of Selenite but you may choose one to your likeing. While charging in sunlite is common, during full Moons is considered the greatest source of energy and spiritual connection.

Some look to Witches Calenders (can be found online) and perform readings during certain cycles. Again this is a choice readings can be performed when ever you take a need or desire, Sometimes going days or month between readings to see the development of a path.

Disclaimer

As we have said what you do with the information provided and how you interpret the Runes is deeply personal and must always be done with a level of caution. Only the etchings are set in stone, the meanings are as fluid as life itself.

Now begin your journey

The Sun

The Sun is the dawning of a new day, it brings light and warmth to the lands and those its shines upon. This is the Rune of new beginnings, as the sun rises over the horizon, so does new opportunity and prosperity. Now is the time to begin now projects and see things in a new light.

The Moon

The Moon represents the elements of change that happen in life.
Just as we do not choose how the moon shows itself to us, we
are not always able to decide what changes may occur. To some
this is hard and unyielding, but the changing of the moon is
dependable and as such knowing that we cannot always decide
how things change, we can always be certain that they will.

Flight

As the wind moves across continents so too does the information and people of the world, flight represents communication, travel and all things that move near and far. Is there a trip you've been waiting on? a message that needs sent? A coffee chat and catch up that is long overdue? Now is the time to act on this and go the distance.

The Rings

The Rings symbol is all about the bonds that we make in life, not just the commitment of matrimony. We share bonds with friends, pets, parents sometimes even distant strangers through online activities, this is reminding us to lean on those bonds in the times we need it most. It's hard sometimes to go through situations and feeling these links can be a comfort that although we feel separated, we are never alone.

Romance

Romance is as described, it represents the irrefutable bonds of love and reaches into the depths of companionship as we try to find our twin flames. Perhaps there is someone in your life already or you are considering a relationship with someone close, this rune is encouraging you to take the dive at something further and take the next step that you both need.

The Woman

The Woman represents the motherly gift that embraces all children young and old. You feel its warmth, healing and comfort knowing that times can be hard but in her light, all things are not as bad as they seem. Perhaps there is a figure in your life that radiates this presence, this rune tells you to go to them and let them help you through whatever strife is before you.

The Man

The Man represents all things masculine, strong and most importantly fatherly. A father shields his family from the cold and protects from the physical dangers ahead, while their hands are callused and rough their touch is gentle and safe. This is about finding the person who will help you face your fears or fight them for you, you will stand tall because they won't let you do otherwise.

The Harvest

The Harvest is the time when all the hard work of the year
has paid off and fruits of labour have now come to bare. As
you have tended, nurtured and sacrificed for your goal you
may now reap the rewards of this conquest. But do not sit
back and ignore the work still to be done, as the rewards
maybe enjoyed a farmer does not rest knowing the new crop
is to be sown and as such you must not be complacent.

Crossroads

The fork in the road, the T in the junction, the indecisions of life laid out and no indications of where to turn. Crossroads can be a frustrating rune as it lays bare the issues brought forward by having either to much choice or no where to turn. When this rune shows up it is asking you to think before acting, maybe take a step back and wonder does the path have to be a straight choice or can I move between them, or maybe avoid them entirely.

The Star

A shooting star is said to grant wishes and with that in mind we set the goals of life by what we wish for the most. The Star is about the hope and desires we set for ourselves, we see them burn brightly in the distances but by always seeing the light we know the direction that we need to strive. Like the sailors of old using the north star to guide them you can use this moment to guide yourself and others where you need to be.

Waves

As the oceans of the world are pulled by the moon this rune reflects the idea that things will happen outside of our control. Waves crash into the shoreline then recede just like the turbulences of life, once we accept this then we can allow bad times to flow over and away from us as water often does. Do not become overwhelmed by the waves, where needed step back and remember that diving deeper holds dangers even to those best prepared.

The Scythe

The Scythe is the blade that cuts deep, being a tool of harvesting or a weapon to defend yourself. This Rune is about the cutting of ties allowing one to move on and begin a new. We must cut the harvest before beginning the new season, a new crop cannot take root while the old lingers. Sometimes there is someone in our life holding use back or even causing us harm, this rune tells us that now is the time to cut these ties and strike out at new opportunities.

The Eye

The Eye is all about revelation and truth, the pulling back of the veil often spiritually, sometimes figuratively and sometimes practically. It asks us to look closely to the reveal the secrets kept from us or simply look deep enough that our own truths are revealed. Perhaps a revelation is on the horizon and you aren't paying close enough attention, this asks you to now take the steps that will allow clarity and understanding.

TARRANT HATTER

Breaking down the Reading

Its important not to jump to conclusions, often after a reading we are propelled into questions and revelations about our current situation. Always take a step back and view as an outsider where possible.

Would a future happen if we didnt know how it would happen?

Will it happen this was if we choose not to act?

All questions to consider before making any decisions

We hope you have enjoyed this book and will continue your study. The translations and meanings we have given are open to everyone's interpretation and reading elsewhere will show you, further, deeper and elaborate interpretations that will guide you further.

If you don't have a rune set yet check out our website
www.hatterskreations.com
to purchase your first set and begin your Divination journey.

Printed in Great Britain
by Amazon